Islamic Culture

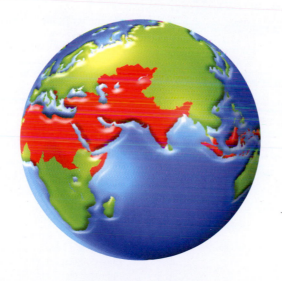

Charlotte Guillain

Heinemann
LIBRARY

Chicago, Illinois

www.capstonepub.com
Visit our website to find out more information about Heinemann-Raintree books.

To order:
☎ Phone 800-747-4992
🖷 Visit www.capstonepub.com to browse our catalog and order online.

Edited by Charlotte Guillain, Abby Colich, and Vaarunika Dharmapala
Designed by Steve Mead
Original illustrations © Capstone Global Library Ltd 2013
Illustrations by Oxford Designers & Illustrators
Picture research by Ruth Blair

Originated by Capstone Global Library Ltd
Printed and bound in the United States of America in North Mankato, Minnesota.
062015 009003RP

17 16 15
10 9 8 7 6 5

Library of Congress Cataloging-in-Publication Data
Guillain, Charlotte.
  Islamic culture / Charlotte Guillain.
      p. cm.
  Includes bibliographical references and index.
  ISBN 978-1-4329-6779-6 (hb)—ISBN 978-1-4329-6788-8 (pb) 1. Islamic civilization. 2. Islam. I. Title.
  DS35.62.G85 2013
  305.6'97—dc23   2011037703

Acknowledgments
We would like to thank the following for permission to reproduce photographs: Corbis pp. 5 (© Anthony Asael/Art in All of Us), 13 (© David Bathgate), 15 (© Franz-Marc Frei), 19 (© Caren Firouz/Reuters), 21 (© Ken Cedeno), 22 (© Jashim Salam/Demotix), 23 (© EPA), 25 (© Kazuyoshi Nomachi), 26 (© M.K. Chaudhry/EPA), 27 (© fotographer/Demotix/Demotix), 31 (© Hunter), 32 (© Peter Turnley); Getty Images pp. 8 (David Sutherland), 11 (Andy Sotiriou), 12 (Steve Raymer), 28 (David Silverman), 29 (Syamsul Bahri Muhammad), 34 (EIGHTFISH), 35 (Michael Heffernan), 36 (Turkey Tigers/Bloomberg); Photolibrary pp. 6, 7, 10, 20, 39; © Photoshot p. 30; Photoshot pp. 18 (© World Pictures), 24 (© Xinhua); Shutterstock pp. 16, 43 bottom right (© manzrussali), 17, 43 top right (© mehmetcan), 37 (© Dimitrios), 41 (© ImageTeam), 43 top left (© S.Borisov), 43 bottom left (© J. van der Wolf), design features (© muharremz).

Cover photograph of a smiling African boy reproduced with permission of Corbis (© Pascal Deloche/Godong). Cover design feature of colorful tiles reproduced with permission of Shutterstock (© muharremz).

Every effort has been made to contact copyright holders of any material reproduced in this book. Any omissions will be rectified in subsequent printings if notice is given to the publisher.

CONTENTS

Some words are shown in bold, **like this**. You can find out what they mean by looking in the glossary.

INTRODUCING ISLAMIC CULTURE

What do you know about **Islam**? Maybe you are a **Muslim** or you have Muslim friends? You might have read about the religion of Islam or heard about Islamic people on the news.

Islam is one of the world's major religions, and it has followers across the globe. Islam began in Arabia. Muslims believe the **Prophet** Muhammad received a message, known as the **Qur'an**, from Allah (God). Muhammad shared this message with others, and the religion of Islam quickly spread.

The countries where Islam is found today are in the Middle East, northern and eastern Africa, and Central and Southeast Asia. Millions of Muslims live in other countries, too. There are different groups of Muslims, such as Shi'a, Sunni, and Sufi. However, the basic beliefs of Islam are shared by all.

What is culture?

Culture includes the values, beliefs, and attitudes of a particular group of people. It is about how they live and worship and about the music, art, and literature they produce. Islam has a very distinctive culture.

Did you know?

'Ilm means "knowledge." Many important scientific discoveries were made in the Islamic world, and studying has always been an important part of Muslim culture.

ARCHITECTURE AND ORNAMENT

Islamic art and **architecture** often reflect religious beliefs. For example, Muslims usually avoid showing people and animals in their artwork. **Traditionally**, powerful Islamic rulers employed artists, craftspeople, and architects to create beautiful objects and buildings. The results of their work can be seen across the Islamic world.

Architecture

Mosques, where Muslim people worship, are among the most stunning Islamic buildings. Other Islamic architecture includes palaces, fortresses, and homes.

The stunning Süleymaniye Mosque in Turkey has many domes and minarets.

Mosques were built as places for Muslims to meet and pray together. The first mosques included features such as a central courtyard and porches in the north and south walls. Later mosques built for powerful rulers, such as the Umayyads based in Syria, were more complicated. Features such as the **minaret**, a tall tower from which Muslims are called to prayer, and the *mihrab* were added. The *mihrab* is a niche in the mosque wall to show Muslims which direction to face as they pray.

Many mosques and other monuments have huge domes, such as the Dome of the Rock in Jerusalem. Inside, decoration can include colorful painted tiles and beautiful **calligraphy**.

Here you can see inside the Dome of the Rock in Jerusalem. It is decorated with geometric patterns and writing.

The Prophet Muhammad (c. 570–632 CE)

The Prophet Muhammad preached the central message of Islam: there is no God but God, and Muhammad is the messenger of God. He lived in Makkah, in present-day Saudi Arabia, but he moved to the city of Madinah in 622 CE, to avoid being killed by his enemies.

Gardens

Islamic culture developed in the hot, desert countries of the Middle East, Turkey, India, Spain, and North Africa. People built cooling gardens from the 900s CE onward.

Types of garden

Gardens are important in Islamic culture. They offer a cool and peaceful refuge from the heat and bustle of city life. People can use them as a place to reflect and think about Paradise, as it is described in the Qur'an.

The Qur'an describes Paradise as a garden. Many Islamic rulers tried to reflect this by creating beautiful gardens in their homes and palaces.

Larger Islamic gardens are called *bustan*, and they were often built as part of palaces. They usually included pools and streams of water surrounded by trees and plants. In more impressive gardens, such as at the Alhambra in Spain, a layout called *chahar bagh* (meaning "four gardens") was used. This involved a central fountain, with four water channels flowing out into the four sections of the garden.

Traditional homes in cities such as Damascus, in Syria, often have hidden courtyard gardens that cannot be seen from the street. Residents can enjoy the shade of these private gardens, which usually feature a fountain.

Other gardens were created to remember the dead. One of the most famous is at the Taj Mahal in India. This *chahar bagh* garden was built by Shah Jahan, with his dead wife's tomb set at the top of the garden, facing the central pool.

Shah Jahan (1592–1666)

Shah Jahan was a ruler of the Islamic **Mughal Empire** in India. He was a powerful emperor who was interested in the arts and had many mosques and monuments built.

The Taj Mahal is the most famous of Shah Jahan's buildings. It is known around the world for its beauty and harmonious design. It was built to remember the favorite of his three queens, Mumtaz Mahal.

Modern Islamic gardens include the Al-Azhar Park in Cairo, Egypt, which opened in 2005. It makes use of traditional Islamic features such as geometric patterns, lush greenery, fountains, and waterways.

Painting

Although pictures of people are discouraged in Islam, a tradition of portrait painting began in Persia (present-day Iran) in the 1500s. This spread to the Mughal and Turkish Ottoman empires. Rulers paid artists to paint portraits and natural scenes. Riza Abbasi was a famous Persian artist who created small paintings, called miniatures, of people in gardens. In the Mughal Empire, many books were illustrated.

In the 1900s, painting flourished in Iran, with artists such as Muhammad Ghaffari starting an art school. Today, modern Islamic painters include Ali Omar Ermes and Ahmed Moustafa. The Indonesian painter Abdul Djalil Pirous wants his paintings to show that he can be a good Muslim by creating art.

Glass and ceramics

Glassmaking became common in the Middle East during the 600s CE. Islamic craftspeople found new ways to decorate and shape glass, and these traditions continue in Egypt today. Many glassmakers produced lamps specifically for mosques, usually decorated with calligraphy.

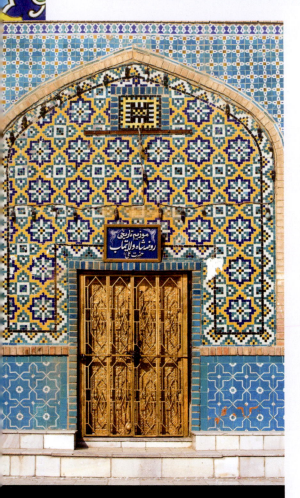

Painted ceramic tiles are often decorated with geometric patterns or mosaics. Tiles decorate many mosques and palaces.

Islamic craftspeople have used clay to make **ceramics** for centuries. Lusterware is a type of ceramic that developed in Iraq in the 800s CE. Lusterware is pottery painted with a metallic sheen.

This Egyptian glassblower is making a perfume bottle.

Calligraphy

In Islam it is believed that the word of God was revealed to the Prophet Muhammad. Because of this, the way those words are recorded is very important to Muslims. **Scribes** wrote down the messages Muhammad was said to have received from God in the first Qur'an, using Arabic calligraphy.

Calligraphy is a style of writing that makes words look beautiful, while also recording them for people to read. Many ancient manuscripts were decorated with gold and colored paint. Copying out the **script** is still seen to be an honorable and religious act, so calligraphers are greatly respected.

The Arabic script in Islamic calligraphy uses different letters from those in the English alphabet.

Calligraphy is used to decorate mosques and other Islamic buildings. It can also be found on many paintings, tiles, and other ceramics. The writing is usually text taken from the Qur'an.

Calligraphy today

Many Muslims learn how to write Arabic script following the rules of calligraphy. Professional calligraphers use pens made from reed (tall grasses with stems) or brushes. They learn to write in different scripts, and their training can take years.

Hassan Massoudy (born 1944)

Hassan Massoudy is a calligrapher from southern Iraq. He loved art, but he grew up in a town where images were discouraged. He became interested in calligraphy instead. He studied Arabic calligraphy in Baghdad during the 1960s, before going to art school in Paris, France. Over the years, his calligraphy has become more important than his other painting.

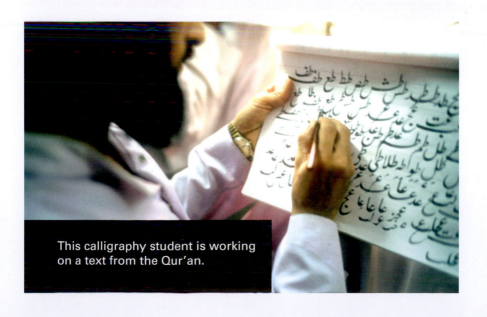

This calligraphy student is working on a text from the Qur'an.

PERFORMANCE

Some Muslims find performances of music and dance unacceptable. Many followers of Islam only allow music in religious settings, such as chanting the Qur'an and the call to prayer. Other Muslims feel their beliefs allow them to enjoy music, while some use music to feel closer to God.

Classical Islamic music

Classical Islamic music started in the courts of ruling families. Musicians usually created new music as they played. This is known as improvisation. Qur'anic recitation is performed by an unaccompanied voice. But most music in Islamic culture is accompanied by other voices or instruments. Musicians focus on the beat and play around with the tune.

Different parts of the Islamic world have their own traditional style of classical music. In Turkey a classical concert is called a *fasil*. Performances have been held for centuries, both for rulers in palaces and in public places. Traditional Persian music is called *dastgah*. It became established in the 1800s and has changed very little since.

Farida Mohammad Ali (born 1963)
Farida Mohammad Ali is a classical singer from Iraq. She sings traditional *maqam* music with the Iraqi Maqam Ensemble, a group of musicians. She has won awards for her singing and performs around the world.

Islamic instruments

Similar instruments are played across the Islamic world. These include cymbals, drums, and tambourines. These instruments usually accompany wind instruments, such as the *zorna*, the *urghul*, or *zammarah*. There are also string instruments, such as the *al-'ud*, which looks like a guitar with a short neck, and the *ganun*.

These musicians in Tanzania are playing a style of music called *taarab,* which blends Islamic and African cultural influences.

Did you know?

Zapin is a type of dance that has spread around the world alongside Islam. The dance began in the Middle East, but it is popular in Malaysia today. The musicians accompanying the dance usually include singers. Originally *zapin* was a folk dance that anyone could join, but today it is mainly performed for an audience.

Dance in Islamic culture

Not everyone in Islam approves of dance, particularly for women. For others, such as the traditionally **nomadic** desert Bedouin, folk dance is an important part of their culture. Bedouin music and dance are usually based on traditional stories passed down through the generations by performance.

Folk dance

There are many other types of Islamic folk dance, such as the *bar* in Turkey. These dances are performed outdoors by groups of men or women. The dancers stand side-by-side and link arms as they dance. The *dabke* is a traditional dance in Lebanon that is performed to celebrate the harvest.

Sufi dancing

Sufis are a group of Muslims, many of whom live in Turkey. The Mawlawi order of Sufis are famous for their dancing, which is performed by men called dervishes. The dancers wear brown, cone-shaped hats with long white robes. They dance in a large hall, where they also live together.

The dervishes' whirling dance helps them feel closer to God. They dance for spiritual reasons, rather than for entertainment.

Storytelling

There has always been a strong tradition of storytelling in Islamic culture. The Hadith are traditional teachings given by the Prophet Muhammad. These teachings were passed on and shared, creating a tradition of **oral** storytelling. For centuries the *hakawati*, or storyteller, was an important entertainer in the Middle East. *The Thousand and One Nights* is a well-known collection of stories from this region. Today, storytellers are less common, because television and the Internet are the main forms of entertainment for many people.

Puppets and plays

Puppet shows have traditionally been popular in many Islamic countries. In Turkey a type of shadow puppet show called *karagöz* is well known. Puppeteers hold up flat puppets behind a sheet lit by an oil lamp. The characters usually argue, and then a story is told.

Some *karagöz* puppeteers have a different story for each night of the month of **Ramadan**.

These Iranian actors are part of a group of Muslims called Shi'a. They are reenacting an important battle from their history.

In the past, groups of actors mimed (acted without words) to entertain Islamic rulers. The Ottoman rulers enjoyed performances whenever they held a celebration. In the Middle East and North Africa, open-air theater was often performed, including shadow plays. Other Muslims watched **passion plays** once a year. In Iran these religious plays are called *ta'ziyah*. They show tragedies from Islamic history. Actors perform the plays over 10 days at the start of the Islamic year.

BELIEFS AND FESTIVALS

The religion of Islam is central to Islamic culture around the world, with certain beliefs and festivals shared by all Muslims. Some Muslims interpret the Qur'an and the teachings of Muhammad differently from others. Behavior and **customs** can vary from place to place.

YOUNG PEOPLE

Many Muslim children go to Qur'an school, or *madrasah*, at their local mosque. They are taught to read and memorize the Qur'an in Arabic, and they also learn about the life of the Prophet Muhammad and the customs of their religion.

Many Muslims give money to charities such as the Red Crescent. This money is used to help people around the world.

The five pillars of Islam

The five pillars of Islam are the ways in which Muslims can follow their religion properly. They are like rules for leading a good life.

The ritual of washing before prayer is called *wudu*.

+ *Shahada* is a profession of faith or declaration of belief, in which Muslims say, "There is no God but Allah and Muhammad is his prophet."
+ *Salaat* is prayer. Muslims should pray five times a day, starting at sunrise and finishing at night. There are special **rituals** before Muslims pray. For example, people wash their hands, face, and feet. Prayers in the mosque at noon on Friday are especially important. When they pray, Muslims face toward the holy city of Makkah (also spelled Mecca).
+ *Zakat* is giving money to the poor and others who need help.
+ *Sawm* is **fasting**. Muslims do not eat or drink from dawn to sunset during the holy month of Ramadan.
+ *Hajj* is **pilgrimage**. Muslims are supposed to make a pilgrimage to Makkah during their lifetimes.

Ramadan

Muslims believe that the word of God was revealed to the Prophet Muhammad during the ninth month of the Islamic year. This month is called Ramadan, and it is considered very holy. The Qur'an tells Muslims to mark this holy time by fasting from dawn to sunset for 29 to 30 days.

Muslims get up before dawn to eat and drink enough to give them energy for the day. They fast until the sun sets and then eat a light meal. Later in the night, a larger meal is shared. Muslims fast to be "mindful of God" and keep Allah in their thoughts. They are willing to give up food and drink, since they believe Allah commands this. Many Muslims spend more time reading the Qur'an and praying during Ramadan, especially in the evenings.

The pre-dawn meal during Ramadan is shared among family and friends.

'Id-ul-Fitr

At the end of Ramadan, Muslims celebrate 'Id-ul-Fitr. People give money to the poor to help them celebrate, too. The celebration begins when the new moon is seen and a new month starts. Muslims dress up and go to the mosque to pray. Then, a special meal is shared. Many people decorate their homes with lights.

YOUNG PEOPLE

Children under the age of about seven are not expected to fast during Ramadan. Older children join in the fasting, but they may not fast for the whole month until they are teenagers. Muslim children look forward to 'Id-ul-Fitr, when many receive new clothes, sweet treats, or gifts of money.

'Id-ul-Fitr is one of the happiest times in the Islamic year.

Hajj

The city of Makkah, in present-day Saudi Arabia, is a holy place for Muslims. The Qur'an says that the Prophet Ibrahim (also spelled Abraham) built the first house for worshiping God there. All Muslims who are well and wealthy enough try to make a pilgrimage, or *Hajj*, to Makkah.

During *Hajj*, **pilgrims** have to live in a special way, called *ihram*. They must not argue or fight, and they do not wear any jewelry or perfume. Men wrap two white sheets around themselves, while women wear a plain dress. Everyone wears simple sandals or walks barefoot.

Did you know?

'Id-ul-Adha is the festival that takes place at the end of *Hajj*, when Muslims around the world celebrate. Traditionally, an animal is **sacrificed** and a third of the meat is given to the poor. Muslims get together to share food and many give presents.

Over a million pilgrims travel to Makkah each year for *Hajj*.

Arrival in Makkah

When pilgrims arrive in Makkah, they go to the Ka'bah, a cube-shaped building in the center of the city's Great Mosque. Muslims believe the Ka'bah is on the site of the house of worship built by Ibrahim. The pilgrims circle the Ka'bah seven times and hurry between two hills. They travel to the plain of Arafat, where they pray in the open. Next, they sleep outside for one night, before going on to throw stones at a stone pillar at Mina. Here, they sacrifice a sheep or goat and cut their hair, before going back to the Ka'bah and circling it another seven times.

Pilgrims try to touch the Ka'bah as they circle it.

Islamic New Year

The Islamic New Year is called the Day of the Hijrah. Muslims believe this date marks the time that Muhammad left Makkah and went to live in Madinah (also spelled Medina) in 622 CE. This date is remembered by Muslims because when Muhammad made this journey, the religion of Islam began to spread. Many Muslims mark this day by sharing stories about Muhammad.

Did you know?

In the Islamic calendar, each new month begins at night, when there is a new moon. Each month lasts 29 or 30 days, so the Islamic year is shorter than the standard calendar. This means that Ramadan, *Hajj*, and other festivals happen during different seasons over time.

These people in Pakistan are celebrating Muhammad's birthday, 'Id Milad-ul-Nabi.

These candles have been lit for prayers on the eve of Lailat ul-Qadr.

Lailat ul-Miraj

Lailat ul-Miraj celebrates the night that Muslims believe Muhammad journeyed to heaven and was taught by Allah. They believe that this was when Muhammad was told that Muslims should pray five times a day. People around the Islamic world mark this day by reading the Qur'an and saying special prayers.

Lailat ul-Qadr

The Night of Power is known as Lailat ul-Qadr. This night falls toward the end of Ramadan. It marks the night Muslims believe Muhammad heard the first words of the Qur'an. Some Muslims spend several nights reading the Qur'an.

FAMILY AND COMMUNITY

Family and community are very important in Islamic culture. People take care of their relatives and try to be friendly to others around them. Important events such as births and weddings are shared with the whole community.

A new baby

When a baby is born to a Muslim family, he or she is washed and dressed, and then the father whispers the *adhan* (call to prayer) into the baby's right ear. Some Muslims rub sugar, honey, or a crushed date onto the baby's gums or tongue. This custom shows that the parents want the baby's life to be sweet and good.

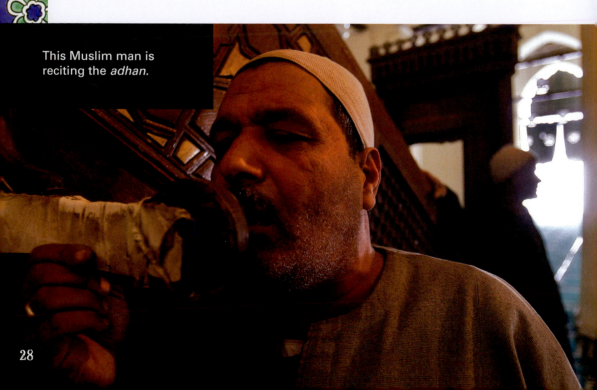

This Muslim man is reciting the *adhan*.

Soon after the baby is born, a **ceremony** called *aqiqah* is held. This is a naming ceremony in which friends and relatives gather to hear the baby's name.

Bismillah

Some Muslims celebrate Bismillah around the time a child is four. The child starts to learn certain verses from the Qur'an in Arabic and how to say them correctly. He or she also starts to learn how to pray. Around this age, most Muslim children start going to Qur'an school, or *madrasah*, at the mosque.

YOUNG PEOPLE

Khatam al-Qur'an is a celebration held when a child can recite the whole Qur'an from memory. When this happens, guests are often invited to a dinner and the child receives gifts.

Marriage

Traditionally, Muslim families have tried to find suitable partners for young men and women to marry. Today, in many places, it is more common for young Muslims to find their own husband or wife. Both the bride and groom must agree to the marriage.

Wedding traditions

Muslims living in the United States might celebrate a wedding in different ways from Muslims in North Africa or Indonesia. However, many Muslims around the world still wear traditional wedding clothes. Before the ceremony, the groom must give the bride a gift, and sometimes the couple's family and friends give them money. The wedding itself often takes place in a family home, with readings from the Qur'an and prayers. Sometimes an **imam** or a marriage officer (*ma'zoun*) is present.

When a Muslim couple marries, their two families are also seen as joining together.

In all Islamic weddings, the bride and groom must agree to a contract, called a *nikah*, setting out the conditions of their marriage. They are only considered married when this contract is agreed to and witnessed. A celebration called a *walimah* follows, including a large meal with family and friends.

Did you know?

In some countries and traditions, there are lavish preparations for the bride before a wedding. She may have a special bath and sit among burning incense, to smell beautifully perfumed. Often her female friends and relatives join her to talk about her married life that is to come.

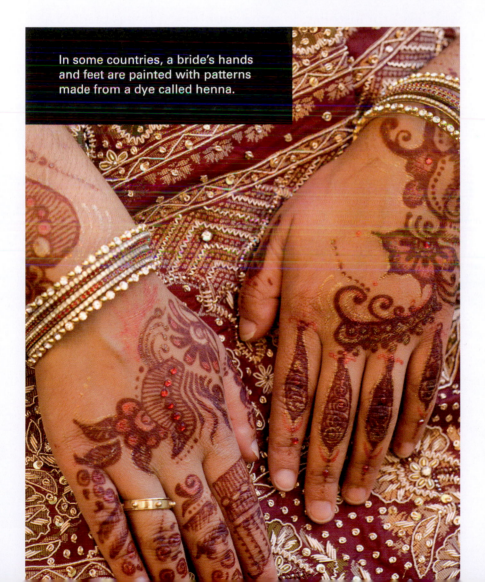

In some countries, a bride's hands and feet are painted with patterns made from a dye called henna.

Death

When Muslims know a friend or relative is close to death, they help them ask God for forgiveness and to say or hear the *shahada*, or declaration of faith, before the person dies. The dead person's relatives wash the body and sometimes put perfumed oil onto the skin. Then, the body is wrapped in special white cloth. If the dead person went on *Hajj*, this could include the clothing he or she wore there.

A funeral prayer called Salaat al-Janazah is said before a burial. Where possible, Muslims are buried facing Makkah. In most places, Muslims do not mark their relatives' graves with large tombstones. In some countries, a tree is planted at the grave.

All Muslims are buried after they die. Burial happens as soon as possible after a death.

Remembering the dead

For three days after a death, there is a period of **mourning**. Visitors come to see the dead person's family and bring food. In some Islamic communities, people wait for 40 days and then hold a gathering to remember the dead person. Friends and relatives may stay up together overnight, reading the Qur'an and praying. The following day, they may share a meal. All Muslims remember the dead by visiting their graves.

Did you know?

Muslims believe that a dead person's soul returns to God. When Muslims hear of a death, it is common for them to say, "To God we belong and to him we will return." They believe that their lives on Earth are just the start of their journey. Because of this, many Muslims try to live good lives and ask for forgiveness for any wrong they have done before they die.

Life after death

Followers of Islam believe that one day Allah will bring life on Earth to an end. All the people who ever lived will then be judged by Allah. Those who did good things will go to Paradise. Paradise (Jannah) is described in the Qur'an as a garden, full of happiness and comfort. Muslims believe those who have done bad deeds will go to hell for punishment.

CUSTOMS AND ACTIVITIES

Muslims follow special rules, called *adab*. These rules tell Muslims how they are expected to behave in their lives.

Many Muslim women cover their head, body, arms, and legs.

Clothing

In Islamic culture, both men and women are expected to dress **modestly**. They keep parts of their bodies covered in public and wear loose-fitting clothes. In Pakistan, men and women wear *shalwar-qameez*, a long, loose shirt and pants. In Saudi Arabia, men traditionally wear a long robe with a scarf called a *keffiyeh* or *shemagh* on their heads. Some Muslim women cover their heads with a scarf, or *hijab*. Others wear a long gown, called an *abayah* or *burqa*, and a veil over their faces called a *niqab*. Many Muslim women choose not to cover their heads and instead wear Western-style clothing.

Men and women

Traditionally, Muslim women have managed the home and raised children. The husband's role was to provide what the family needed. In some parts of the Islamic world, this is still normal. In those places, Muslim women spend most of their time in the family home, only going out with a male relative. In other places, Muslim women go out to work and lead independent lives outside the home.

YOUNG PEOPLE

In most Muslim communities, young girls do not cover their heads. Children usually dress modestly, but girls are only expected to start wearing a *hijab* when they become teenagers. Some young boys wear traditional Islamic clothes when they go to the mosque. This can include a cap called a *taqiyah*.

These Muslim men are wearing robes called *kanzu* and hats called *kofia*.

Food

The rules that Muslims are expected to follow regarding food are set out in the Qur'an. Food they are allowed to eat is called *halal*, while food they are forbidden to eat is called *haram*.

Haram foods and drinks include any meat from a pig, animals that have not been killed in the proper way, and alcohol. *Halal* meat comes from animals that are killed in the proper way. This involves saying a blessing while the animal's throat is cut. Many Muslims buy meat from special *halal* butchers, where it is correctly prepared.

These Muslim men are drinking coffee at an outdoor café in Turkey.

Sharing meals

In Islamic culture, it is important to show friendliness and hospitality toward visitors. Many Muslims share a meal with visitors. Often Muslims wash their hands and say a prayer or pronounce God's name before they eat or drink anything.

In some countries, families will serve their guests first and keep offering them more food until they are full. Only then will the family start to eat. In some countries, it is the custom to eat from shared plates, using the fingers. It is usual to eat with the right hand, as the left hand is used for personal hygiene.

Did you know?

Typical dishes in Islamic countries include *halva,* a dessert that is made of seeds and nuts. In the Middle East, a sweet pastry called *baklava* (see photograph) is made with honey and nuts. In Morocco a meat stew flavored with dried fruits such as apricots is a famous dish. Popular drinks include sweet mint or lemongrass tea and spiced coffee.

Games

Many different games and sports are played in Islamic countries and communities. One strategic game is played using a wooden board with cup-shaped indentations and some small stones. It can also be played on the ground without a board. The players have to think ahead several moves and capture their opponent's pieces. This game is called *bao* in East Africa, *congklak* in Indonesia, and *mancala* in Turkey.

Karam is another popular board game, and it is thought to have originated in India. Players try to knock discs into pockets in the corners of a large board. Many people play this game in East Africa, the Middle East, Pakistan, and Bangladesh.

Sports

Some Muslims are limited in the sports they can play because they strictly follow the Islamic rules of modesty. However, many Islamic communities enjoy playing sports such as **cricket**, soccer, and field hockey.

Imran Khan (born 1952)

Imran Khan is a Pakistani politician who played international cricket for over 20 years. In 1992, when he was captain of the Pakistan team, the team won the cricket World Cup. Today, he works hard to improve the lives of people in Pakistan.

In India, Pakistan, Afghanistan, and Iran, many people enjoy flying kites. There are kite-flying festivals in which people display colorful and detailed kite designs. Kite-running is also popular in these places. Traditionally, players try to cut their opponent's string using crushed glass on their own kite string. However, this has now been banned in some countries for safety reasons.

These people are celebrating
a kite-flying festival in Pakistan.

ISLAMIC CULTURE IN THE 21ST CENTURY

As Islamic culture has spread around the world, it has changed and adapted to include the customs and daily lives of many different people. While some Muslims follow the Qur'an and what is expected of them in a strict and controlled way, others believe their lives as Muslims can be more open and relaxed.

Many members of the global Islamic community are proud of their culture and heritage and are eager to show their beautiful artwork, architecture, and music to the rest of the world. They are proud to be part of a culture that has always encouraged learning, led the way with scientific discovery, and created beautiful art.

Did you know?

Muslims around the world use the same greeting when they meet each other. It is polite and respectful to greet people by saying, "*As-Salamu 'alaikum*," which means "Peace be upon you." The reply is "*wa alaikum as-Salam*," which means "and on you be peace."

While the center of Islam remains the Middle East and North Africa, there are now Muslims in many countries who share a belief in the values of their religion and culture. Although they may dress differently from one another and celebrate festivals in a variety of ways, most Muslims respect the family and the wider Islamic community, and they try to live their lives in a modest, polite, and friendly way. Festivals such as Ramadan bring the worldwide community of Muslims together, allowing them to pass on their faith to new generations.

This building is the Burj al Arab, located in the United Arab Emirates. It has become a striking symbol of modern Islamic culture.

TIMELINE

CE

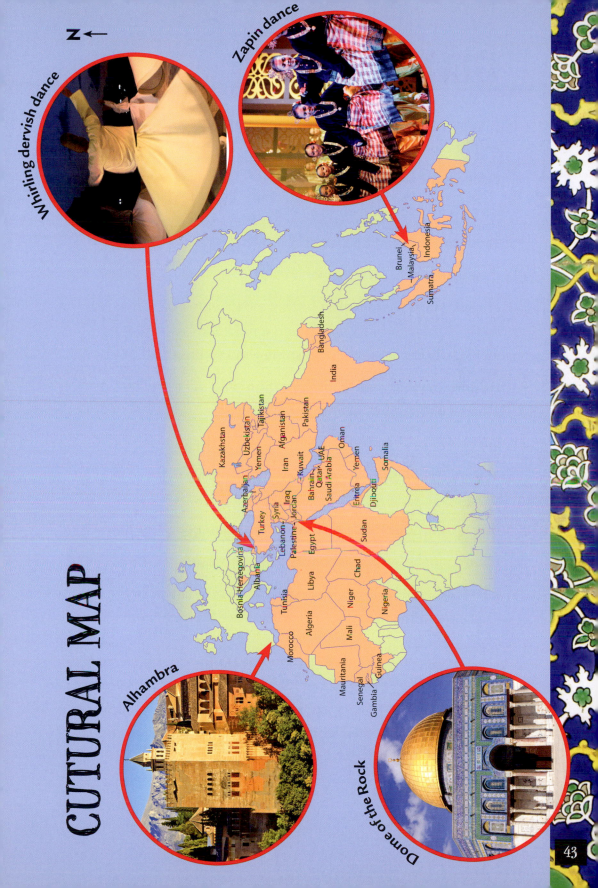

CUTURAL MAP

N

Whirling dervish dance

Zapin dance

Indonesia
Brunei
Malaysia
Sumatra

Bangladesh

India

Pakistan

Kazakhstan
Uzbekistan
Tajikistan
Afganistan
Yemen
Iran
Kuwait
Oman
Azerbaijan
Qatar UAE
Yemen
Bahrain
Saudi Arabia
Somalia
Turkey
Iraq
Eritrea Djibouti
Syria
Lebanon Jordan
Bosnia-Herzegovina
Palestine
Egypt
Sudan
Albania
Libya
Chad
Tunisia
Niger
Nigeria
Morocco
Algeria
Mali
Mauritania
Senegal Guinea
Gambia

Alhambra

Dome of the Rock

GLOSSARY

architecture design of buildings

calligraphy decorative handwriting

ceramics objects made from clay

ceremony acts and behavior on an important occasion

classical artistic, traditional music

cricket sport that involves hitting a ball with a bat. Two teams with 11 players each compete on a field with two markers called wickets. It is similar in some ways to baseball.

culture customs, social organization, and achievements of a particular nation, people, or group

custom way things have been done for a long time

empire group of countries ruled by a single government or ruler

fast go without food or drink for a certain period of time

imam person who leads prayers in a mosque

Islam religious faith of Muslims, based on the text of the Qur'an and the teachings of the Prophet Muhammad

minaret tall tower from which the call to prayer is made

modest way of dressing and behaving that is considered proper and decent

mosque building in which Muslims meet and worship

mourning expression of sorrow after someone's death

Mughal Muslim rulers who controlled a large part of India and modern-day Pakistan between 1526 and 1848

Muslim person who follows the religion of Islam, which began in Arabia in the 600s CE

nomadic describes people who move from one place to another, usually in search of grazing land for animals

oral spoken

passion play play showing religious events

pilgrim person who goes on a pilgrimage

pilgrimage journey to a holy place that is important in a religion

prophet religious teacher

Qur'an holy book of the Muslims

Ramadan month in the Muslim calendar when Muslims fast from sunrise to sunset every day

ritual formal actions in a ceremony

sacrifice when something is offered to God, often a slaughtered animal

scribe person who writes things down

script style of handwriting

symbol sign

tradition customs that are passed on from one generation to the next

FIND OUT MORE

Books

Blashfield, Jean F. *Pakistan* (Countries Around the World). Chicago: Heinemann Library, 2012.

Brownlie Bojang, Ali. *India* (Countries Around the World). Chicago: Heinemann Library, 2012.

Milivojevic, Jovanka JoAnn. *Afghanistan* (Countries Around the World). Chicago: Heinemann Library, 2012.

Nardo, Don. *The Islamic Empire* (World History). Detroit: Lucent, 2011.

Toor, Atif. *Islamic Culture* (Discovering the Arts). New York: Newbridge Educational, 2006.

Websites

https://www.cia.gov/library/publications/the-world-factbook/index.html
The World Factbook has country profiles with information on geography, people, and more. Learn more about the countries mentioned in this book at this website.

kids.nationalgeographic.com/kids/places/find
Search for Afghanistan, Egypt, Iran, Iraq, Morocco, and Turkey to find photos, videos, map, and activities.

www.lacma.org/islamic_art/islamic.htm
Learn more about Islamic art—from ancient times to the present—at this website of the Los Angeles County Museum of Art.

Places to visit

The Freer Gallery of Art and the Arthur M. Sackler Gallery, Washington, D.C.

www.asia.si.edu

The Freer and Sackler Galleries contain many important examples of Islamic art.

The Los Angeles County Museum of Art, California

www.lacma.org

The Los Angeles County Museum of Art has an impressive collection of Islamic art.

Metropolitan Museum of Art, New York City

www.metmuseum.org

The Metropolitan Museum of Art has 15 galleries that follow the history of Islamic civilization from Spain in the west to India in the east.

More topics to research

What topic did you like reading about most in this book? Did you find out anything that you thought was particularly interesting? Choose a topic that you liked, such as food, buildings, or religion, and try to find out more about it. You could visit one of the places mentioned above, take a look at one of the websites listed here, or visit your local library to do some research. You might be able to visit your local mosque with your class. You could try playing a game of *bao* or *karam* or try some *baklava* or *halva*!

INDEX